Level 2

The Nature Kid's Guide to
GIRAFFES

RENATA MARIE

LP Media Inc. Publishing
Text copyright © 2023 by LP Media Inc.
All rights reserved.

No part of this book may be reproduced or transmitted in any form or by any means, electronic or mechanical, including photocopying, recording, or by an information storage and retrieval system — except by a reviewer who may quote brief passages in a review to be printed in a magazine or newspaper — without permission in writing from the publisher.

For information address LP Media Inc. Publishing,
3178 253rd Ave. NW, Isanti, MN 55040
www.lpmedia.org

Publication Data

Giraffes
The Nature Kid's Guide to Giraffes — First edition.

Summary: "Learn all about Giraffes, the Nature Kid Way"
— Provided by publisher.

ISBN: 978-1-954288-66-9

[1. Giraffes – Non-Fiction] I. Title.

Title: The Nature Kid's Guide to Giraffes

CONTENTS

Up and Up! 4
Long Necks 6
Hard to Spot 8
Leafy Eats 10
Ewy Chewy 12
Eat. Eat. Eat! 14
Hidden Danger 16
Kick It! 18
Neck-Out Round 20
Standing Sleepers 22
Long Way Down 24
Cute Kickers 26
Tall Towers 28
Snorts and Roars 30
Tipping Towers 32
Less Land 34
Hunted 36
Looking Up 38

UP AND UP!

A long neck reaches up, up, up! A giraffe eats yummy leaves.

Giraffes live in Africa. The land is dry. Tall grass grows. A lot of animals eat the grass. But giraffes can eat more than grass. **Their long necks help them eat tree leaves.** But that is not all their necks can do!

FUN FACT! Giraffes are the tallest land animals.

LONG NECKS

A giraffe stands tall. His legs are long and thin. His neck is just as long!

Male giraffes can be 18 feet (5.5 meters) tall and weigh up to 3,000 pounds (1361 kilograms). Female giraffes can be 14 feet (4.3 m) tall and weigh up to 1,500 pounds (680 kg). **Their necks can reach six feet (1.8 m)** and weigh 600 pounds (272 kg). That is a long neck!

FUN FACT!

Most humans are shorter than a giraffe's legs.

A giraffe walks beneath a tree. His spots make him hard to see.

Giraffes use **camouflage**. **Their fur is full of spots.** The spots look like shade under trees. They look like leaves. Being hard to spot is important. It keeps giraffes safe from **predators**.

DID YOU KNOW?

There are different types of giraffes. Some have tan fur. Others have almost black hair. What a giraffe eats and where it lives makes its fur the color it is.

LEAFY EATS

Wild Apricot Leaves

Acacia Leaves

Mimosa tree Leaves

Lick! **A giraffe uses his long tongue to pick leaves.**

Giraffes are **herbivores**. They mostly eat leaves. But they also eat flowers, small branches, and fruits.

Their favorite food is the leaves of acacia trees. The tree has sharp **thorns**. Luckily, giraffes have even longer tongues. They easily reach around the thorns and get their tasty treats.

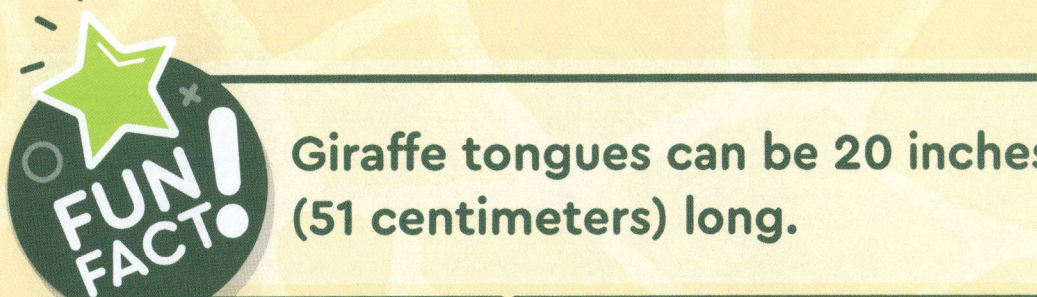

Giraffe tongues can be 20 inches (51 centimeters) long.

EWY CHEWY

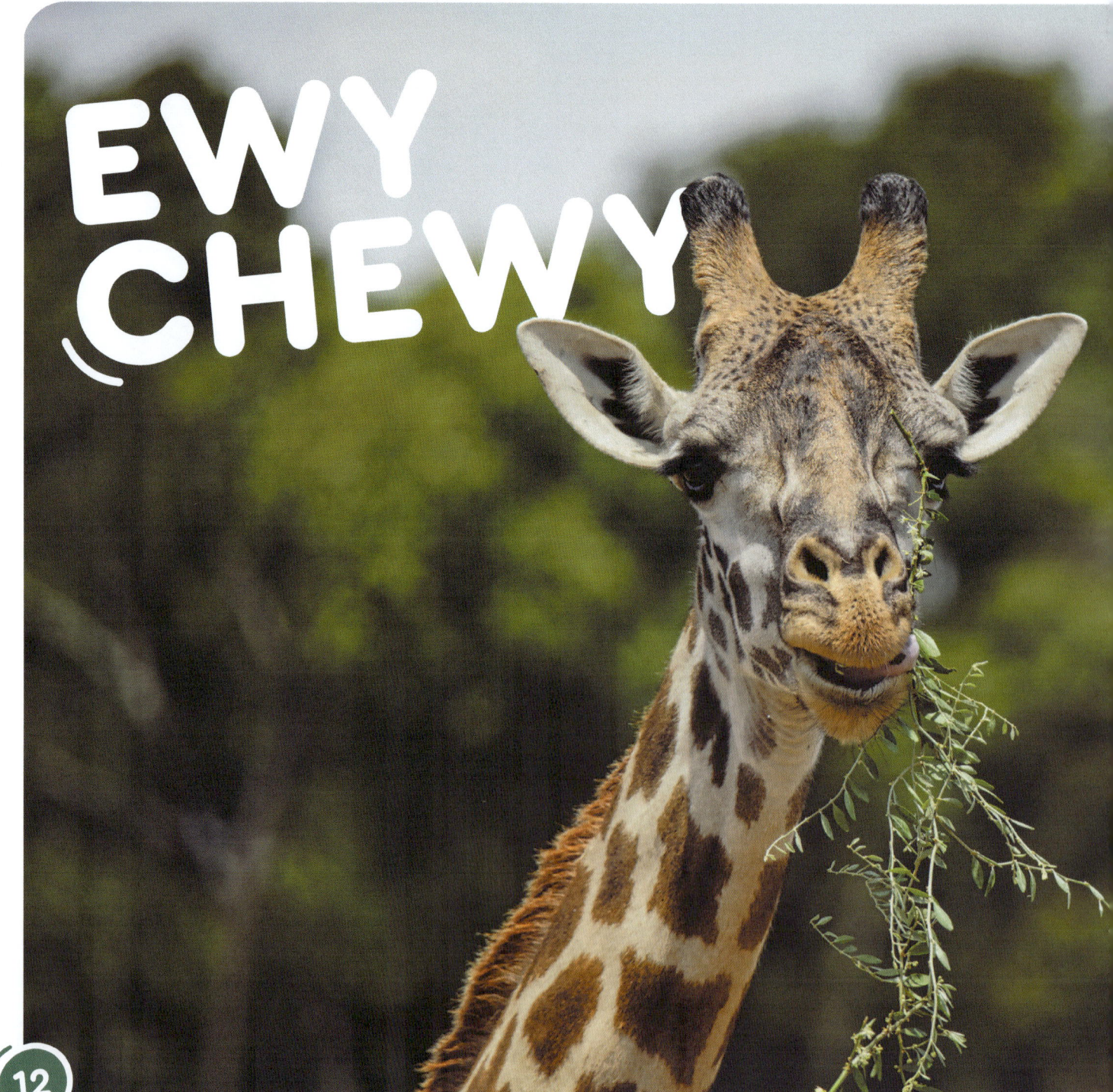

A giraffe throws up its food and chews it again.

Leaves are hard to eat. Giraffes swallow them. Then the leaves come back up to their mouths. **Giraffes chew them over and over again.**

They also have a lot of spit. The spit coats their food. It makes it easy to swallow. Even thorns.

FUN FACT! Giraffe stomachs have four parts, just like cows.

The sun dips low, but the giraffe keeps eating.

Giraffes only get a few leaves with each bite. **They eat 75 pounds (34 kg) of food each day.** It takes them most of the day to eat all of that food.

Leaves give giraffes a lot of water. They only need to drink every few days. But when they do, their necks have a long way to bend.

DID YOU KNOW? Giraffes have lips that can reach around thorns.

HIDDEN DANGER

A giraffe lowers her head to drink, but she has to be careful. Predators may be hiding nearby.

Crocodiles can spring from the water. Lions, hyenas, and leopards can charge on land.

Giraffes watch over each other while they drink. Their eyes are sharp. Their height helps them see far.

FUN FACT! Giraffes can drink 10 gallons (38 liters) of water a day.

Leopard

Hyena

Lion

Crocodile

KICK IT!

A lion charges a giraffe. But the giraffe will not go down without a fight.

Giraffes stick close together. It makes it hard for predators to hunt them. Sometimes predators get one alone. **Giraffes use their long legs to run fast.** They run at 35 miles (56 kilometers) per hour.

And if that doesn't work, they kick—hard.

DID YOU KNOW? Giraffe feet are 12 inches (30 cm) wide. That is the size of a dinner plate.

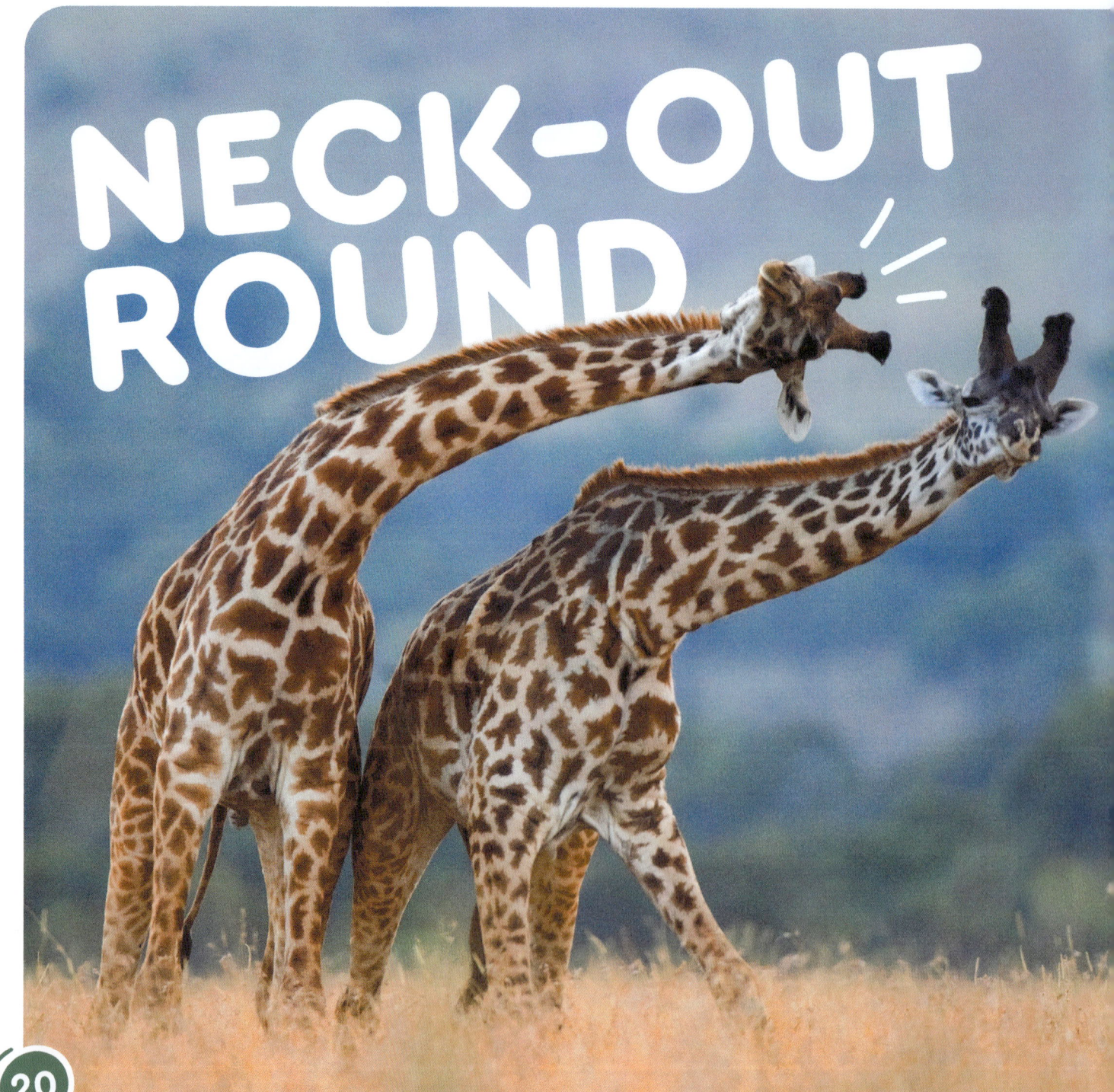

NECK-OUT ROUND

Smack! **A male giraffe swings his neck. His horns hit another male giraffe.**

Male giraffes do more with their necks than reach for food. **They use them to fight other giraffes.**

All giraffes grow bumps. The bumps look like horns. Males use their horns to battle. The battles are called "necking." They want to see which giraffe is stronger. The stronger giraffe might win the female's attention.

DID YOU KNOW? Male giraffes can grow three horns. They can even grow five horns.

STANDING SLEEPERS

A giraffe rests her head. She is fast asleep.

Giraffes are quick sleepers. They only sleep 30 minutes a day and in short naps. **It is too dangerous to be asleep for a long time.** While a giraffe sleeps, another giraffe will watch out for predators. Staying safe takes teamwork.

FUN FACT! Giraffes can sleep standing up.

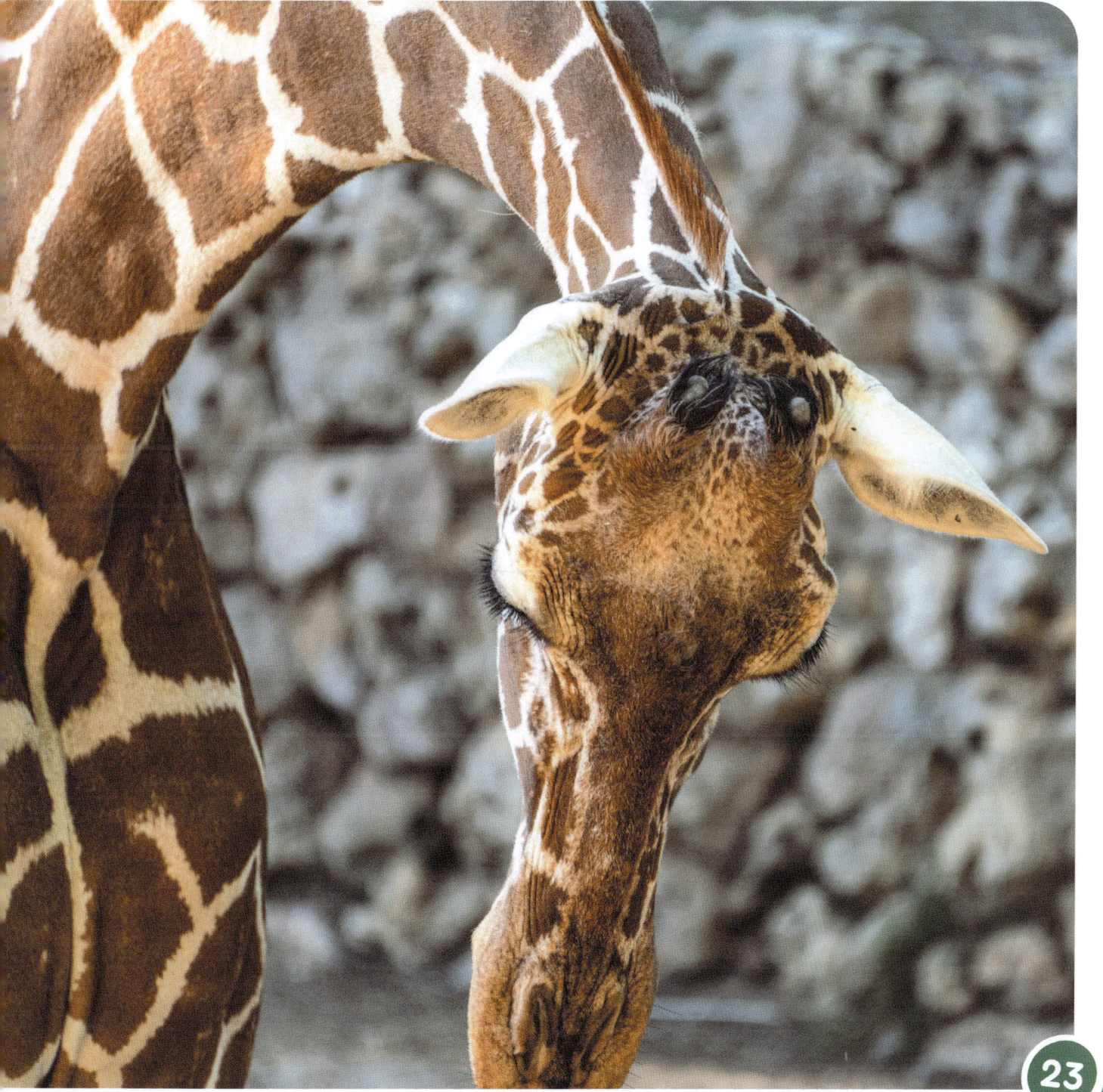

Thud. A baby giraffe is born.

Giraffes do not just sleep standing up. They give birth standing up. That is a long way to fall.

Baby giraffes are called calves. The fall does not hurt them. But predators could. They have to learn to run quickly. In 30 minutes, calves can stand. Their legs wobble. In an hour, they can walk. And soon, they can run.

Giraffes give birth standing up, so their calves' long necks are not hurt.

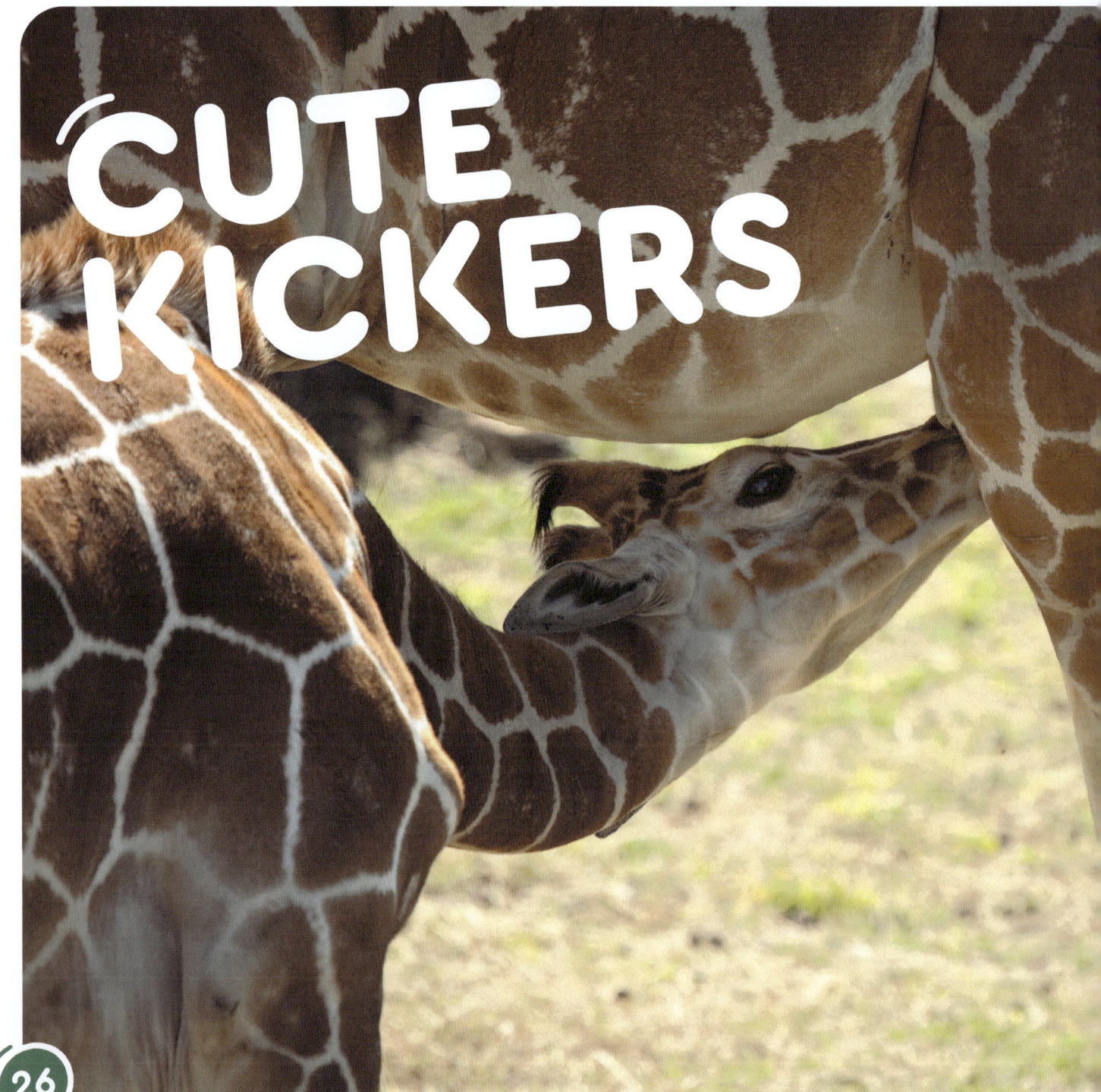

CUTE KICKERS

A calf reaches her neck up.
She drinks milk from her mother.

In a week, calves start to eat plants. Their mothers take turns watching the calves. **The calves play together.** They run. They kick. They jump. The calves grow strong. They learn to be friends. This is important for animals that live together.

DID YOU KNOW?

Calves are six feet (1.8 m) tall when they are born. In their first week, they grow one inch (2.5 cm) each day.

TALL TOWERS

A male giraffe stands tall. He leads the giraffes to more trees.

Giraffes live together. **There are about 20 giraffes in one group.** Each group is led by a male giraffe. The rest of the giraffes are females or calves. When male calves grow up, they leave the group. They find other males to live with.

FUN FACT! A group of giraffes is called a **tower**.

SNORTS AND ROARS

The lead giraffe snorts. A hyena is nearby.

Giraffes snort when they see predators. They want to warn the other giraffes.

Giraffes are quiet animals. **But they make other noises too.** Calves bleat and mew. Female giraffes bellow to find their calves. Giraffes moo and grunt. They hiss, whistle, and hum. They even roar.

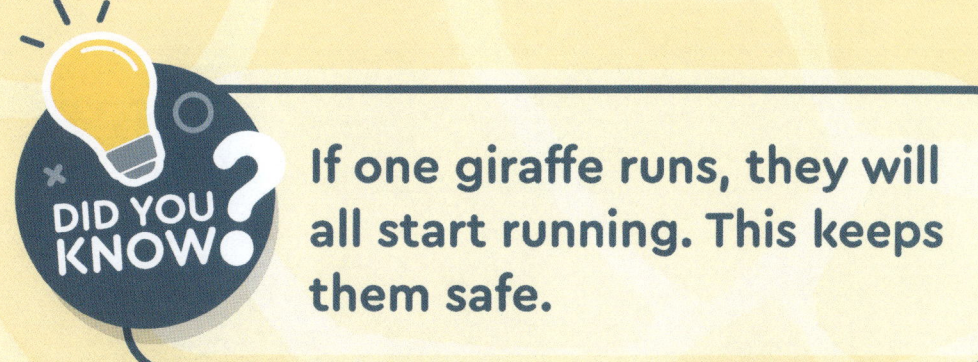

If one giraffe runs, they will all start running. This keeps them safe.

TIPPING TOWERS

A giraffe looks over his home. He does not see a safe land.

Giraffes used to see trees and grass all over Africa. Now, they see farms, roads, and houses. Giraffes are **endangered** animals. There are only about 100,000 giraffes left in the wild. **What happened to the giraffes?**

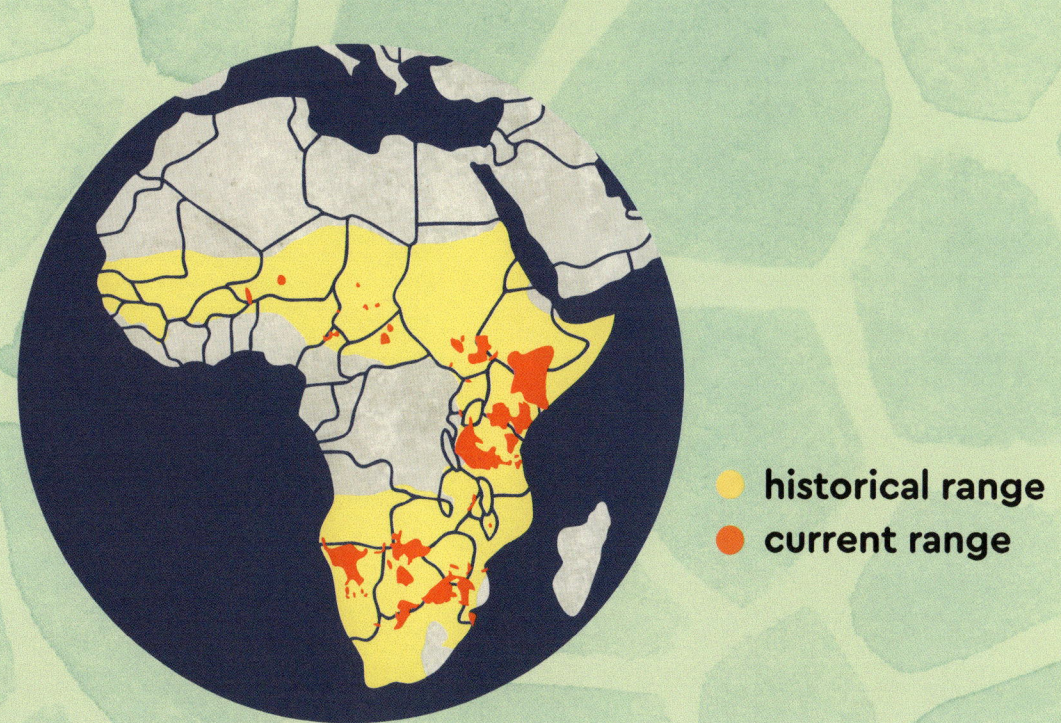

- historical range
- current range

LESS LAND

A giraffe looks for food, but the farm animals beat him to it.

Humans built towns. They built roads and farms. Giraffes now have less land. There is less food to eat, and farm animals are not helping. They eat the plants. They leave little food for wild animals.

Giraffe land is broken up. It is hard for males to find females. Fewer calves are born.

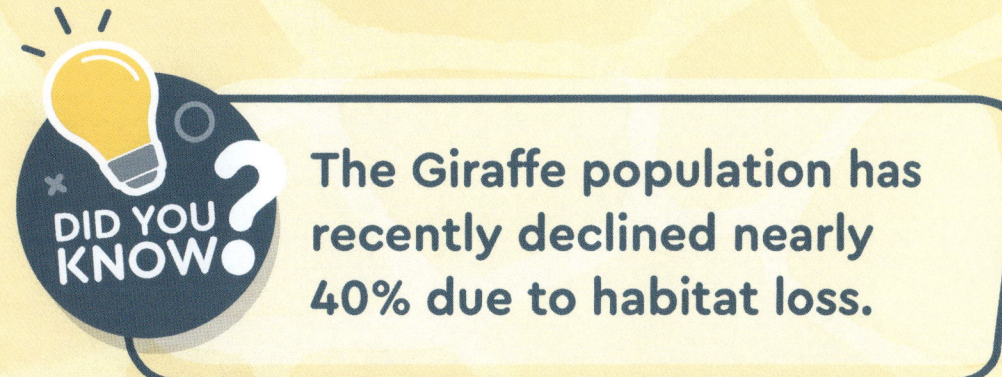

The Giraffe population has recently declined nearly 40% due to habitat loss.

HUNTED

A gun blasts. A giraffe snorts. They run.

Some people hunt giraffes illegally. They shoot giraffes or catch them in traps. They want to sell giraffe skin and fur. They want to sell their tails and meat. Some people hunt giraffes for sport. Others use their tail hair to make bracelets. They use it to sew.

Each giraffe has different spot markings.

LOOKING UP

A giraffe spots an acacia tree. It is new. The giraffe runs over.

People are planting trees. They want to regrow the giraffes' favorite trees. **They want their land to be full of food.** Then the giraffes will stay away from farms.

People are watching out for illegal hunters. They are stopping them. They want the giraffes to live peacefully. Then the giraffes can stand tall once more.

DID YOU KNOW? In the US, nearly 600 giraffes live in zoos

GLOSSARY

camouflage
something that helps an animal hide
page 9

predators
animals that hunt other animals
page 9

endangered
in danger
page 33

thorns
a sharp part of a plant
page 11

herbivores
animals that eat plants
page 11

horns
bumps that come out of an animal's head
page 21

tower
a tall, thin building
page 29

MORE AMAZING ANIMAL BOOKS
from Nature Kids Publishing!

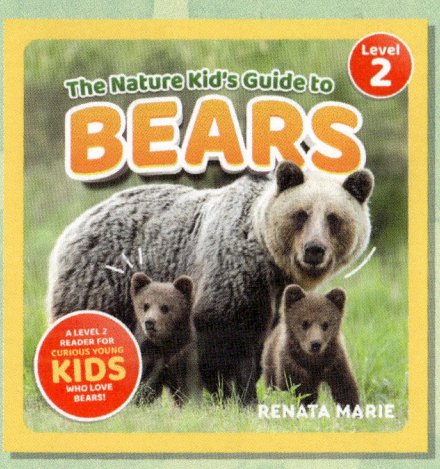
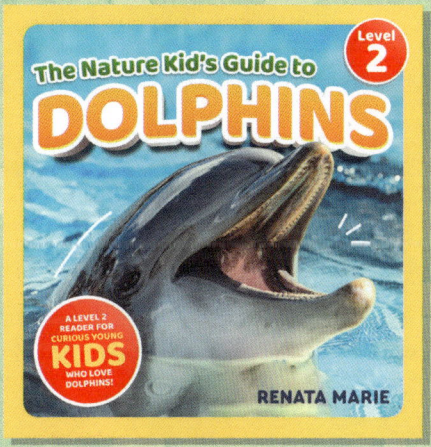

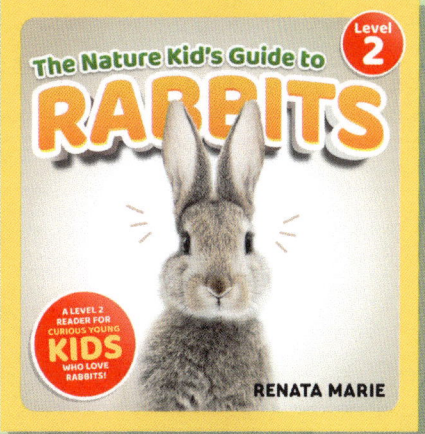

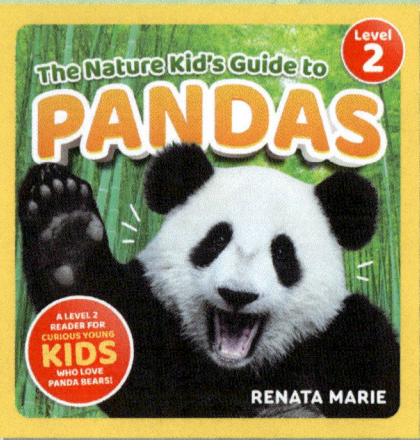

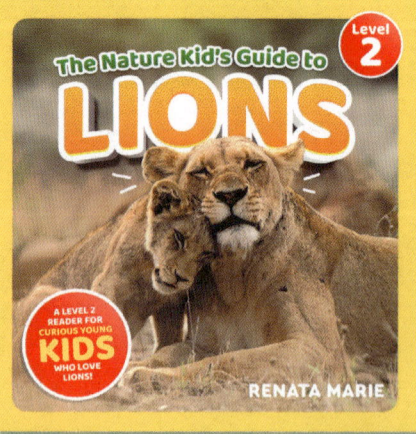

Visit NatureKidsPublishing.com to Learn More!

Printed in Dunstable, United Kingdom